PELVIS WITH DISTANCE

PELVIS WITH DISTANCE

A BIOGRAPHY-IN-POEMS/
SELF-PORTRAIT BY PROXY

JESSICA JACOBS

WHITE PINE PRESS / BUFFALO, NEW YORK

WHITE PINE PRESS
P.O. Box 236   Buffalo, New York 14201
www.whitepine.org

Acknowledgments:
I would like to thank the editors and staff of the following publications,
in which these poems, sometimes in different forms and with different
titles, first appeared.
Beloit Poetry Journal: "The Shelton with Sunspots"
The Burden of Light: Poems on Illness and Loss: "Sky Above Clouds VI"
Cave Wall: "The Grey Hills," "Road to Pedernal," "In the Patio IV (Black
Door)," "In the Canyon II (Fear/Breaking)," and "In the Canyon V
(Memory)"
Common-place: "To Find You" (poems I-IV)
Acknowledgments continue on page 137,
which constitutes an extension of this copyright page.

Publication of this book was made possible, in part, by grants from
Amazon.com and with public funds from the New York State Council
on the Arts, a State Agency.

Cover art: Alfred Stieglitz. *Georgia O'Keeffe — Neck 1921*. The
Metropolitan Museum of Art. Gift of Georgia O'Keeffe, through the
generosity of The Georgia O'Keeffe Foundation and Jennifer and Joseph
Duke, 1997 (1997.61.19). Copyright © The Metropolitan Museum of Art.

First Edition

ISBN: 978-1-935210-66-5

Printed and bound in the United States of America.

Library of Congress Control Number: 2014947459

For my parents, Lauren Goodman and Harry Jacobs.

Every day I am grateful to be your daughter.

TABLE OF CONTENTS

In the Canyon I (Arrival) / 15

I.

Red Barn in Wheatfield / 19
Alfred Stieglitz at 291 (First Encounter) / 21
Untitled (Dead Rabbit with Copper Pot) / 23
Sent August 14, 1915 / 24
Early Abstraction / 25
No. 8—Special (Palo Duro Canyon with Spiral) / 26
In the Canyon II (Fear/Breaking) / 27
To Find You (Georgia O'Keeffe Museum) / 29
Coney Island, 1917 / 31
Sent June 6, 1917 / 33
Nude Series VIII / 34
Music—Pink and Blue II / 35
In the Canyon III (Love) / 36

II.

To Find You II (On Stieglitz's Photos of O'Keeffe) / 39
Self-Portrait in Absentia / 40
Georgia O'Keeffe (Half-Naked, in White) / 42
Plate 28 (Clothed in Only a Swim Cap) / 44
In the Canyon IV (Reflections) / 46
Lake George, 1922 / 47
Alfred Faces the Camera, Georgia Turns Away / 48
Sent 1926 / 50
The Shelton with Sunspots / 51
Wave, Night / 53
An American Place Exhibition Catalogue
                    (The Flower Paintings) / 54
In the Canyon V (Memory) / 56

III.

Sent in the Summer I / 59

From the Faraway, Nearby / 61

In the Canyon VI (Hallucinations) / 62

Sent in the Summer II / 64

The Grey Hills / 65

Sent in the Summer III / 67

Road to Pedernal / 68

In the Canyon VII (Everyday) / 70

Sent in the Summer IV / 72

Black Abstraction / 73

To Find You III (Georgia O'Keeffe Museum Research Center) / 75

Pelvis with Distance / 77

In the Canyon VIII (False Starts) / 78

Sent Early 1940s / 80

Pedernal, 1945 / 81

Sent April 18, 7:30 a.m. / 82

July 13, 1946 / 83

Sent July 10, 1946 / 85

IV.

A Black Bird with Snow-Covered Red Hills / 89
The White Place in Shadow / 91
In the Canyon IX (Loneliness) / 92
In the Patio IV (Black Door) / 94
Sent August 4, 1950 / 95
In the Patio VIII (Green Door) / 96
In the Canyon X (Uncovering the Mirrors) / 98
To Find You IV (O'Keeffe's Abiquiu House) / 99
Composite [Self-]Portrait as Wise Desert Elder / 100
Sent August / 101
Georgia O'Keeffe, by Alfred Stieglitz (Composite Portrait) / 102
In the Canyon XI (To the Poet) / 104
Sky Above Clouds IV / 106
Once in Her Eighties Georgia Attempts a Joke / 108
To Find You V (Questions for Georgia) / 109
Like an Early Blue Abstraction / 110
In the Canyon XII (Last Run) / 112
May 6, 1986 / 113

Selected Bibliography / 115
Notes / 117
Acknowledgments / 131

PELVIS WITH DISTANCE

For phrases and images throughout the collection I am indebted to Georgia O'Keeffe's writings in *Georgia O'Keeffe* and *Some Memories of Drawings*, the letters of O'Keeffe and Alfred Stieglitz, and Laurie Lisle's *Portrait of an Artist: A Biography of Georgia O'Keeffe.*

All poems whose titles begin with "Sent" are excerpts from actual correspondence.

All poems in the voice of O'Keeffe or Stieglitz respond to a painting or photograph named in the poem's title and further identified in the Notes.

I decided to start anew—to strip away what I had been taught, to accept as true my own thinking. This was one of the best times of my life . . . I was alone and singularly free, working into my own unknown—no one to satisfy but myself.

—Georgia O'Keeffe

By a series of strippings such as this one enters the desert.

—Barry Lopez

IN THE CANYON I (ARRIVAL)

[Abiquiu, NM; present day]

From the outside, the cabin is a small adobe butte: thick-walled and squat, with a roofed wooden deck that doubles its claim of desert. The shower, a black bag, dangles from a beam, and the outhouse, two minutes' walk to the west, is a toilet on a platform with no walls. Inside—tight as a ship's hold—a window punched into each white stucco wall. There's no electricity, no reception. On the only set of shelves, the food I hope will last a month, which is how long I am to live here.

This morning—a life ago—the gray ribbon of highway fissured a thousand variations of red. From Santa Fe past pueblos of single-wides, scrawny dogs minnowing the heat-shimmers. Past the taquerias and feedstores of Española and onto 84. A stretch long and straight enough to invite excessive speed, it's marked with descansos of makeshift crosses, flowers, and toys—an alternate triptik of lost children and travelers who died without reaching their destinations.

Then sixteen miles of rutted dirt road, the flat top of Pedernal hovering above—the mountain Georgia O'Keeffe painted obsessively, half-joking that God told her if she painted it often enough it would be hers.

To write these poems, I've come to live in her backyard.

At the ranch, I park in a back pasture. Transfer books, food, and my dog into the caretaker's beat-up black truck. The final five miles are more tire tracks than road, helixed so tight to a riverbed—mostly dry in this driest June—we cross it thirteen times before leaving one canyon to enter another. Beyond a scumble of scrub brush and low-slung piñons, the cabin.

This noon sun devours all shadows. Only questions remain.

15

I.

RED BARN IN WHEATFIELD

O'Keeffe
[Sun Prairie, WI; 1892]

The drays were kept out in the heat
all day. So were we: my cheek pressed

to flanks dark with sweat,
watching their sides twitch, rippling curtains

of flies—the closest I got then to seeing
the sea. I licked salt from my lips

as though fresh from the water, but nothing
was better beneath bare feet

than horse-shadowed earth
threaded with pine needles. Air so thick

with dust I wanted to lie down in it,
to wrap it round me like a cloak

and walk the fields gone tall
with summer, grasshoppers

popping at my step like oil on a flame.
My sisters hid in the creamery, cooled

by ice cut from ponds in winter, playing
Handy Andy Over among the milk cans.

But beside the high hedge, I was happy,
shimmied into the drive's loose gravel,

running my fingers through buggy-cut ridges
until I couldn't help but turn

pebbles on my tongue. Burr of silt. Their shapes
still bloom behind my tight-shut teeth.

ALFRED STIEGLITZ AT 291 (FIRST ENCOUNTER)

O'Keeffe
[New York, NY; 1908]

When that boy demanded I muse for him
—learn the thousand ways

in an unmoving hour
to itch—I sat, the painted not the painter,

until other students intervened, invited
us out to troop through the snow, pure

only in its falling. We tracked
the slurried grit five flights

up to that anonymous box of a room
with drawings by Rodin skewered

to its walls. Sketched with his eyes closed,
they all said, same way Stieglitz must have

hung them. But, then—a negative
dripping from his fingertips—there he was:

a summer thunderstorm in that bricked-in
brownstone. At their questions, the weathervane

of his body began to swivel. No, these are not
a joke; yes, they are art. Even his mustache,

that white whisk broom, bristled. Twice my age
with a bird's nest of hair

and a squash blossom nose—fight-broken,
crooked from the side. And yet.

Yet, my chest clenching as it had
those days storms prowed across the prairies:

by morning, a far darkness, just perceptible;
by noon, a towering freighter

cargoed with magnetic north. He, too,
demanded my attention.

UNTITLED
(DEAD RABBIT WITH COPPER POT)

O'Keeffe, to her friend Anita Pollitzer
[Columbia, SC, to New York, NY; 1915]

In the pines, we found a house,
deserted and crawling
with roses. I came back alone—

a night when the moon made
even the underbrush shine.
Close-grown trees chirred

in the breeze. I locked the door.

Tacked up the paintings
I'd carted from New York
and stared until each

spoke like the teacher
I could see I'd painted it for—
a weak-penciled arm lopped

at the shoulder; Art Nouveau
Virginia lawn; dusky dead rabbit
beside a tarnished red pot—

each painting's tone more
strident than the last, speaking
in every voice but my own.

Anita, I will have to start over.

SENT AUGUST 14, 1915

O'Keeffe, first letter to Stieglitz
[Charlottesville, VA, to New York, NY]

Dear Mr. Stieglitz—

. . . I am the young woman who was so glad to see John Marin make the whole world go crazy. You gave me a 291 number of *Camera Work* and I can't begin to tell you how much I've liked it— I always want it where I can see it in my room—I like it for the things it makes me think of.

Mr. Stieglitz—I want to subscribe . . .

Georgia O'Keeffe

EARLY ABSTRACTION

O'Keeffe, to Stieglitz
[Columbia, SC, to New York, NY; 1915]

They trained us to use our materials as language,
then dictated what we wanted to say.

Unable to paint, I've been slaving for weeks
at the violin. Walking in the woods at dusk each day,

I set my chin to its body. But try as I may
to make music, I just noise to other people's tunes

into the crowns of the trees, which hurl it back,
rooting a forest in my head, with a little found house

inside that. I go there while I play—scrim
the floors with tracing paper. Fear of failure, stone

in my pocket, a measure of charcoal to crawl
these pages. Mother's sweater beneath my knees,

hands smeared black, every angle of my face
traced out, along with the shapes in my head,

which no one had taught me. I wish I could tell you
what I've wanted to say. Instead, here's this drawing.

NO. 8—SPECIAL
(PALO DURO CANYON WITH SPIRAL)

O'Keeffe
[Canyon, TX; 1917]

After the parceled horizons of Manhattan,
Texas plains are a glassy eternity

sealed by a laminate sky. Trapped
between them, I am a too-diluted

pigment, racing
for any edge. Which makes

Palo Duro a deliverance.
At its rim, I am sail,

arms outstretched, ready to crow
over the canyon, dive down into it.

But the only paths in are cañadas,
steep and rocky, forged and rutted

by hoof prints. Straggles of cattle
watch from above, lines of black lace

against the blanched day. By night,
that thrill is still with me. I stand

with brush to the tight-wefted board
while the cows, now penned,

low for their calves,
rhythmic as a Penitente song.

IN THE CANYON II (FEAR/BREAKING)

[Abiquiu, NM; June 2, present day]

Sun lavas over the cliff lip into my first full canyon day while I watch from the marsh of residual night.

When put in touch with the priest who'd lived here for each of the last three Octobers, I'd written to ask how much food to bring, what other supplies.
She'd replied with two questions:

> *What is your experience with solitude?*

> *How are you girding yourself for this time?*

At a sound like a Cessna, I turn to see only a hummingbird.

Pressure builds in my chest.

> I've felt this before,
> but only when confined—
> in a cave's crawl-length, in a crowded tent.
> But here,
> nothing but space,
> but air—for me, for a month, alone.

Knowing the root of anxiety is *anxere*, to be without breath,
I inhale. I try. But breath
is a strangler fig, a ribcage tourniquet. My hands and feet grow honeycombed, carbonated. The dog barks at something only he can see. I ache for a return to bed, for the child's comfort of sheets overhead—*If I can't see this day, it can't see me.*

Rifling books at random, find:

> God, at Creation, poured light into vessels. Unable to contain it, they
> shattered and fell.

> Tikkun olam: Jews gather these shards to repair the world.

But there is a second shattering, a second type of repair:

Tikkun hanefesh, *repair of the soul.*

> Inherent in brokenness
> is breaking open—the ability to hold more than when whole.

How much will I hold when this is over?

TO FIND YOU (GEORGIA O'KEEFFE MUSEUM)

[Santa Fe, NM; present day, a month earlier]

In the great hall, a reliquary: your
navy canvas shoes, jeans,
polka-dotted kerchief. Your voice

from the screening room: *On this knife*
I might fall off on either side. But I'd walk it
again. I'd rather be doing something

I really wanted. There, your resurrected
campsite: canvas-wrapped canteen, Sterno
stove, miniature cast-iron fry pan. Biography

brooded the air. From the gift shop, two men
wore monogrammed chambray shirts "just like
she did." An elderly woman cried in the corner

before the swirl of *White Rose.* And there I was
with these poems. Just that

morning, I'd had to explain, again,
to a friend, that your paintings were more
than postcards writ large; that you both *were*

and *were greater than* your biography.
I was tired. How did you make the choice
to be alone for your art? They'd curated

a corner of your tent up. What would I
make from such loneliness? There was the lip
of your sleeping bag, brown and tan. How

desperately I wanted to crawl in, to rest
for a while in your temporary bed,
to hide, breathing in what you left.

CONEY ISLAND, 1917

O'Keeffe, with Stieglitz

Two-thousand miles from Texas,
this is less an island than Brooklyn

dipping a prim toe into the grime
of Gravesend Bay. It is Decoration Day:

bunting and ticker tape, black-suited
bathers creaking the boardwalk.

Inland, we stroll the midway, where
grease rides the air as ochre foam

rimes the water. There is the tune
and hitch of player-pianos, penny

arcades; barkers touting the ring-toss,
the high-striker. "Two wallops

for a nickel, five for a dime. Win a Kewpie
doll for your cutie pie, an armadillo

basket for her arm." Alfred offers
his arm instead. My fingers notch

in his elbow. The sky turns
cobalt threaded with ivory. Sun full

on my face. With the heat, something
surfaces. We walk; I listen; I talk

when seems called for, but all the while it
rests in my chest: not love, exactly—not

yet—but wanting, purely felt. He touches
my shoulder, steers me to the moment

the diving coaster car meets its shadow,
and my ribs compress around breath,

forming—What? I am back in Palo Duro,
a canvas collecting sack near to tearing

with chalcedony eggs whose outer plainness
belied inner holdings—manganese, copper,

chromium, quartz. The secret to geodes,
though, is to break them. Otherwise: fused

crucible, hollow repository. I watch
his mouth but do not hear what he's saying.

SENT JUNE 6, 1917

Stieglitz, to O'Keeffe
[New York, NY, to Canyon, TX]

. . . And how is the Little Girl—A week ago today was Decoration Day—it seems ages & ages ago—& yet as if but a moment ago— It's as if it had been a dream—it was perfect—that day.—Only much, much too short—It should have included the night.—

You see I never quite get enough of a perfect thing—

NUDE SERIES VIII

O'Keeffe, to Stieglitz
[Canyon, TX, to New York, NY; 1917]

Naked swimmer, I am your
blue lake—a hot moon

lifting from my throat. Tonight,
I am full of wheels and empty

canyons. Desert
so open we walk without

roads. I throw bottles
at the made-to-order stars

for my sister's rifle
to spark, break,

burst glass
to belated sunset.

The sheet on my bed
is a great twist.

It is strange to write you
just because I want to,

but I hate to be undone
by a little thing like distance.

MUSIC—PINK AND BLUE II

O'Keeffe, with Stieglitz
[New York, NY; 1917]

Tonight, I'd paint the world
with a broom

and not be careful
of the floor. Sweep your wife,

your daughter, your any
other women

away. Here,
now, your body

shows me
how to play the notes,

not as written
but as meant

to be played: incantation,
duration, dissolution. Breath,

a circle with two
centers: each

cerulean reservoir; each
a seed syllable—creped bulbs:

vermillion, viridian, byzantium
white. In our hands,

a garden.

IN THE CANYON III (LOVE)

[Abiquiu, NM; present day]

A hummingbird batters the gauzy front curtain, hurling its body at the light.

O'Keeffe wrote to Edna St. Vincent Millay of a similar visitor, "When I had it in my hand it was so small I couldn't believe I had it—but I could feel the intense life . . . You were like a humming bird to me—If you do not understand what I mean your husband undoubtedly will."

At my touch, wings snap in quick as a switchblade. It goes limp.

She continued, "It is a very sweet memory to me—And I am rather inclined to feel that you and I know the best part of one another without spending much time together—It is not that I fear the knowing—It is that I am at this moment willing to let you be what you are to me—it is beautiful and pure and very intensely alive."

Floating my arms out ahead, sweat from the morning's run dried to a tatting of salt across my chest, I walk outside and open my hands. It's gone so fast I don't even feel it lift off.

> All those women I thought I couldn't live without
> whose names I barely remember—
>   is there even one
>   I could write such a letter?

II.

TO FIND YOU II
(ON STIEGLITZ'S PHOTOS OF O'KEEFFE)

Georgia—

>What is it like to be photographed?
>>To be dressed, posed, forced to move or be still?
>
>Does your pose convey a message?
>>If so, is it yours, or one Alfred has given you?
>
>What's it like to look at photos of yourself
>>—right after they were taken?
>>—years later?

Alfred—

>When you meet someone new, how long before you reach
>>for your camera?
>
>Describe
>>—the act of photographing Georgia.
>>—developing those photos, her face swimming up
>>>through the chemical waters.
>
>When looking at each image
>>—do you recall what happened before or after?
>>—can you remember past the frame of the shot?
>
>When shooting, how cut-off or connected do you feel to
>>your subject?
>
>How does a moment change when you begin taking
>>pictures?
>
>How does a person?

SELF-PORTRAIT IN ABSENTIA

Stieglitz, with O'Keeffe
[New York, NY; 1918]

His eye was in him, and he used it on anything nearby. Maybe in
that way he was always photographing himself.
  —O'Keeffe

I see you better than you see yourself.
  —Stieglitz, in a letter to O'Keeffe; 1918

Part that kimono so it frames you like a stage
curtain. Here, on this stool. Slump a bit.

Let's take faces out of it. I'll begin
where your breasts do & end

with your hips. Sag your stomach,
inhale to flatten—no matter;

I control the moment
of exposure. And in my jerry-rigged darkroom

across the hall—while you, in our studio,
remain naked & waiting—I decide

to overexpose the rift
between your thighs, leaving burnt

black absence where a presence
once had been. What lies

in that darkness is mine.

Opening night, I'll wear you
on my arm; spin you like a child

playing pin-the-tail, with you
on every wall. You deny those faces

could possibly be yours, but
glassed and hung in the gallery

they become you—& you, them.

GEORGIA O'KEEFFE
(HALF-NAKED, IN WHITE)

O'Keeffe, with Stieglitz
[New York, NY; 1918]

All down the avenues, summer lakes
the streets. You have bought me

this year in New York, this
studio, whose skylights collect heat

as you do artists—though
I'm the only one you keep

close. Some days it is too much
to wear anything

but this robe, camellia white,
open. When painting,

I am beside
the point. Yet your camera,

that rickety sentinel, draped
in black cloth, waits,

always, against the wall.
Yours in motion

and in stillness. You sold
that photo. Yet here's one

you'll never capture: see this
painting, the height of a man,

and this blur in the middle,
the off-right shimmer?

Reaching to scumble
the too-blue sky, that's where

the breasts you made famous
brushed canvas.

Beneath my clothes, every shade
but your black or white, your gray.

PLATE 28 (CLOTHED IN ONLY A SWIM CAP)

Stieglitz, with O'Keeffe
[Lake George, NY; 1922]

With desire this great, how could sight
suffice? With the eye, everything is over
as it is seen, long-dead by the time

the mind receives it. The camera,
however, is a clock for re-seeing,
stop-bath of the wished-for world:

anyone can see your breast,
half-surfaced, but only I
know a mouth's fit

to the hollows of your collarbone.
Light into platinum negatives
yields print positive revelations:

you in the smell of the off-photo
soil. You, braced against the dock:
atoll of knee, breast, elbow,

and chest, lagoon of the belly,
rib cage's grotto. Ripples of water
up over your neck. Your half-open

mouth. Your gaze, a lens
aimed back at me. The ended instant
perpetually re-begun. With camera

in hand, I am nineteen again, capable
of all your body demands. Look
closely & you will see

the self I want you to be.

IN THE CANYON IV (REFLECTIONS)

[Abiquiu, NM; present day/Wyoming; sixteen years earlier]

At fifteen, I shivered above the Wind River Range treeline, an ellipsis
of rocks rising from a basin of snow, covered by the others' tents.

I preferred to sleep outside. At the base of a Lodgepole Pine, I
stared up through branches curdled in by the wind. No moon
meant stars burning against the blackest sky I'd seen. Alone, snug
in layers of fleece and down, I expanded beyond the confines of my
sleeping bag, beyond the confines of the body wearied and
scorched. I felt connected, part of everything around me, ranging
out, out—until someone coughed in a nearby tent; I retracted back
into myself fast as the tongue of a measuring tape.

Days later, I stood frozen before a truck-stop bathroom mirror: I
couldn't be that dull moon, that reflected flesh. Dirtdark with a
month in the mountains, I'd felt denatured, made new.
      My seen-inside self would not align.
I learned then that our selves require daily recompass.
 For who are we but stories we tell ourselves, stories others tell us,
                                        about ourselves?

The first thing I do in the cabin is cover all the mirrors.

Without them, I grow   transparent as an old-world
photographer's glass plate. My edges   hazy as the noon desert,
salted as a body beneath that zenith sun, until I am prepared
         to slot into the coal black hold   of a moonless night.

Naked in the barrens until morning, I am ready
for what images come with such exposure.

LAKE GEORGE, 1922

O'Keeffe, with Stieglitz
[Stieglitz family summer home, upstate New York]

As it's the only place to be alone, Alfred rows us
    to the middle. I close my eyes not to miss
        the pause in motion
           when the paddles catch, the surge forward
as he draws the oars in, tranquil
    drift of their re-expansion—great wings
           suspended from the oarlocks. It begins
        to rain. His mother lurks a doorway. Alfred turns
toward shore. But I stop his hand, stand, and am
    over. A palm on the gunwale, eyes
        lake-level. In response to each drop,
      the surface sprouts pipettes
of water, a thicket of sudden small shoots.
    Blued banks and mountains
        join their reflections like a zipper,
      trees to trees, dimple and nib. Alfred pulls me back in.

ALFRED FACES THE CAMERA, GEORGIA TURNS AWAY

O'Keeffe, with Stieglitz
[Weehawken, NJ; December 1924]

The ferry churns west across the Hudson.
New York recedes into the fogged
afternoon, Midtown grainy

as a wavering kelp forest. It has begun,
again, to rain. We walk from the dock;
Alfred grips my arm—as a drunk (the phrase

floats in) does a lamppost: for support,
not illumination—all the way to the hardware
store run by the town's Justice of the Peace

where I place shims and a box of nails
on the counter beside our marriage license.
Alfred is not amused. We proceed

to City Hall, which is shrunken as a gallery
between shows. I have taken cold
from the rain. I stand beside him,

nose-stopped, ears-blocked,
the wet of my breath recirculating.
Dimly, I hear "honor and obey."

Dimly, repeat, but my voice
stays behind. Still, it is done.
No rings, no reception. In a hotel,

we make love for the first time
as husband and wife. Alfred sleeps,
a white strait of sheet between us;

maquette of me beneath the sheet, pelvic
escarpments, far hummocks of feet.
Hand behind my head, I stare

at the rippled waves of the ceiling, chart
the stucco crests. His restless body
roils the bed to the roll of water

below a ketch. I'm freed downstream,
beyond the hold of Upper and Lower
Bays, beyond guidance of the West End Light.

When people say, "Mrs. Stieglitz," I will answer,
"Miss O'Keeffe." How little it takes
to make home unfamiliar.

SENT 1926

O'Keeffe, to art critic Blanche Matthias
[New York, NY, to Chicago, IL]

Stieglitz always seems more remarkable—and he brings remarkable things out of the people he comes in contact with—

I feel like a little plant that he has watered and weeded and dug around—

THE SHELTON WITH SUNSPOTS

O'Keeffe, with Stieglitz
[New York, NY; 1926]

You, with your camera, are a boy with a Ball jar,
out trapping fireflies. My secret, though,

is there is no corner I cannot paint
my way out of. You want me as pupil?

Fine; I'm all aperture. All film stock—silver
salted and emulsified. But I won't stop

with just you—I take it all in.
Morning, with its halved-appled light,

exposes in me invisible images,
gray web of water towers,

wind-riffled river—painting calls them out.
Shows how even by day

this is a lunar city. An island of indirect
illumination. I stand to the east and fit

my eye to the grid—New York,
the country's kaleidoscope:

lit/unlit windows,
lumen-tiled towers. Here is where

we live—this gun barrel,
this crested butte, this jack-in-its-pulpit

of smog-hooded sky. And there, in that glare,
our window.

WAVE, NIGHT

O'Keeffe, to Stieglitz
[York Beach, ME, to Lake George, NY; 1928]

Your letter asks how the ocean looks.
It is as terrifically male

and female as ever—shoaling sets
unfolding. There, at the lake,

you train yourself on clouds and carriages—
mastering the wrist flick,

spin of the fingertips—how best to track
and focus. Here, I stand with shifting

tides, mixing pigments quick as I can
to paint line after line on the sand-

propped canvas. I walk up and down
the beach all day,

that blue-ruled primer, copying
a lesson the waves wash away:

Match it exactly and I make it
mine. When you visited,

you watched from the window. Later,
we were benthic, sea-smoothed,

matched: my fingers through your hair
left blue furrows.

AN AMERICAN PLACE EXHIBITION CATALOGUE (THE FLOWER PAINTINGS)

O'Keeffe
[What she wrote/*what she left unsaid*]

Names are just gestures at knowing,
Still—in a way—nobody sees
how children delight in the play of
a flower—really—it is so small—
wind and light
we haven't time—and to see
the great shifting
takes time like to have a friend
the strata of it
takes time . . . So I said to myself—
Then language enters
I'll paint what I see . . .
to transform them
but I'll paint it big
into so many
and they will be surprised
Adams bent on ownership
into taking time to look at it—
through identification,
I will make even busy New Yorkers
adults who keep their heads down
take time to see . . .
preferring lines to colors
Well—I made you take time
whose borders are defined
. . . and you hung all your own associations
by a lack of definition

54

with flowers on my flower
though I'd give myself up to color any day
and you write about my flower
here are some words, though, so we can agree
as if I think and see what you think
—calla, canna, peony, rose—
and see of the flower—and I don't.

IN THE CANYON V (MEMORY)

[Abiquiu, NM; present day]

The mish-mash music station in my mind has finally quit. In the silence, memories surface. All the standard set pieces: awkward break-ups, shameful gaffes, after-the-fact eloquence for occasions long past. And through it all

> the poet from Kentucky, met in the doldrums of a
> New York winter. Five years ago, now. Six?

How the Southern accent she'd unlearned as a kid rose to ghost her syllables when she read her poems aloud.

> How her hair, sun-streaked, was curled as the churning
> waves of a walled-out day on the Pacific.

Her endless gray scarf, unwinding and unwinding as I tried to find my way to her throat.

> The unperfumed warmth in the cleft
> beneath her ear.

The weight of her breasts in my palms as she straddled my hips.

> How I ran after her, out into the
> street, but she'd already left.

Memory as film reel—each image lost to the next so swiftly my eyes lie to conjure broken moments whole.

Flash them past fast enough
> and there she is again in my arms.

III.

SENT IN THE SUMMER I

O'Keeffe; Stieglitz
[Between New Mexico and New York; 1929]

O'Keeffe, May 30:

I wanted to take off my clothes and lie down in the sun naked—
. . . I wonder if you would like me here—I don't know—

Stieglitz, June 8:

Lake George will seem very empty without you—& still I'm glad
you are not going . . . Again I say it's very good you are where you
are. It's the only thing that's right for you—so also for me.

O'Keeffe, June 14:

Last night was moonlight and we took a long drive . . . the terrible
alive sky full of stars—the desert stretching on and on like the
ocean—dark—

Good Night Little One—This seems to be my world—and I can't
help it—

O'Keeffe, June 17:

Dearest—

Tonight there were five letters from you . . . It all sounds pretty
bad—and I know it all so well—

Stieglitz, June: 21

I have been lying about all day—somehow not feeling much like moving about—Just the opposite of you.—All of you alive—all of you—

None of me alive—not even dead.—

Stieglitz, June 24:

. . . Night has set in. For over an hour I have poked the fire—& stood watching *Camera Work* & all else burn.—Five hours of burning. The yellow flames—*Camera Work* burns a marvelous yellow—greet the stars as they appear . . . There are several more wheelbarrows full ready for the flame—I may stay up & burn it all tonight.—Begin the morrow with a cleaner slate— . . . A marvelous cremation . . . I hear my heart beat as if it too were applauding what had been accomplished . . .

FROM THE FARAWAY, NEARBY

O'Keeffe, to Stieglitz
[Abiquiu, NM, to Lake George, NY]

You have not seen it,
so you want me always
to paint flowers. You,

east in the lake house
while I am in the desert,
which is not a place of light

on things but things in
light—a country of form,
of beauty shorn.

There is no middle
ground. Fore
and back collapse

to a single plane.
When I am not here
I am on my way back.

To the scalded hills,
the flare-bleached bones.
To loneliness, calcified.

I paint a deer skull
with too many points,
as though bone could grow

to particular adventure:
I scale the hills, scalp twitching
with velvet of first antler.

IN THE CANYON VI (HALLUCINATIONS)

[Abiquiu, NM; present day]

Hearing is how we touch at a distance.
   —Susan Stewart

The priest heard things and I wonder if I will, too.

Already, everything is sharper: the crab-crawl of pen over paper

    the vireos in the tree to the south, their collective
    song unraveled, each strand tied back to its singer

    audible troughs of air   displaced by the wingbeats
              of low-flying
                hawks.

The rhythmic hum I assume to be me—ventricle whoosh and thump, circulatory hiss.

The tops of the canyon are vertical horizons. Each night, as the sun nears this vanishing, I walk barefoot in the riverbed. The dry sand is peppery and coarse. Stretches that by morning hold a narrow stream, by evening are dry to the eye but have a velvety give—slick and grainy as the mouthfeel of vanilla bean ice cream.

This last light makes the red walls pulse and breathe, everything hazy, ready to be loved on sight. My dog leaps up a bank. I track him through the underbrush by ear.

Then I hear them
        the whispery tintinnabulation of distant bells.

To listen more closely, I stop. They stop
      too, dying seconds after I've ceased to move.
I keep walking, listening, straining to hear where they come from—direction implying a point of origin, an outside source. Finally, I look down.

      With each step, my heel imprints its own small canyon in the sand. When I step away, a scrim of water rises to fill it, disappears in an instant.

That bubbling up is the bell sound.

SENT IN THE SUMMER II

O'Keeffe
[New Mexico, to New York]

O'Keeffe, to Stieglitz, July 2:

. . . I must tell you something else I have done that I haven't
mentioned to you before—The second day I was here at Mabel's
Tony and Beck took me out on the back road and proceeded to
teach me to drive Mabel's Ford—

Well—Tony doesn't laugh readily—but I can tell you he almost
died laughing at me—Four or five days later I got a Ford . . . I
have been driving by myself for about five weeks . . . I didn't want
to tell you till I felt quite safe about it all . . .

The month before, O'Keeffe had written to the photographer Paul Strand:

I just want to tell you I am surviving the Ford . . . I have driven into
the garage twice—and backed out once—the bridges here are only
wide enough for angels to fly over so they give me great difficulty—
but I'm getting on—I broke one window so far—door swung open
when I went through a gate . . .

THE GREY HILLS

O'Keeffe
[Painting in her Model A Ford, New Mexico]

Just past Navajo Country, miles
of malpais. I always go
prepared to camp—tent, stove,

and my valise: oils, drawing sticks,
pastels—you never can tell.
Sand-blasted ventifacts, dunes

like a stiff-tipped meringue.
Gamboge- and saffron-
banded badlands. Off the main

road, pebbles ting the car's carriage,
while clumps of high green ephedra
shush along the doors. Under

the half-shade of a cedar, I lean
a canvas on the back seats, spin
my seat to face it. By four, the bees—

pollen lolling, drunk on color.
Dumb blot of bodies on canvas,
wallow in cadmiums and cobalts,

until they're too encased in paint to fly
or breathe. Still, I envy
their immersion; step

outside. The winds lift
such gales of earth,
they dusk the day. I am sanded

to the recess of every crease
and fold. Return home heavy with it,
set to make a honey of my holdings.

SENT IN THE SUMMER III

Stieglitz; O'Keeffe
[Between New York and New Mexico]

Stieglitz, July 4:

. . . I know the inevitable.—I cannot stop it.—But I know the cure for myself.—These are not idle words.— . . .

The morning mail has come. No letter no sign of life . . .

Again that waiting!

O'Keeffe, July 4:

. . . It is certainly a rare time we are having—Beck and I talked long into the night—Today for the rodeo—and I think the boys intend to dance out there—

We will see—It is the 4th—

My kiss goes through this raw little town— . . .

Stieglitz, July 6:

I had complained about you in minor ways. But my God—I was canonizing you day & night—for thirteen years—as no woman living or in the past was ever canonized . . .

. . . You where you are have no time for such inactivities as these—mine here.—But I live in a land of ghosts—I sleep in a bed of ghost—and the future is blank.—

Without you I am nothing. Without me you go right ahead—will be Georgia O'Keeffe.

ROAD TO PEDERNAL

O'Keeffe, to Stieglitz
[Abiquiu, NM, to Lake George, NY]

In Taos Plaza, vendors ask, "¿Quiere
probar?"—not to taste, but to test
so I often say yes. Insubstantial

as that spun sugar, the view
can be compressed
easy as a hand fan,

folded leaf to leaf: this red
dirt road, washed pink
by spring, doesn't just go toward

the mountain but to it, muscling
up like a great tongue.
Pedernal, in turn, shadows out

to test me. On days when
it is flint, I am the steel
it sparks against. On others,

when I want to rub my face to it
as the deer do my fence posts,
when I grow languid and light

turns into a splendid soft metal, it is
the touchstone that assays me.
I paint it again and again, claiming

and claimed by it. By night,
another transformation:
I seem to become a woman again

and wish to be near you.

IN THE CANYON VII (EVERYDAY)

[Abiquiu, NM; present day]

Three weeks in and canyon life is tidal life. Days wash in and out.

After our morning run, the dog and I sprawl on the porch like petals blown open with heat. Notes and books weighted with stones against the breeze as we edge like hour-hands round the deck, shadow-synced, just beyond the sun's creep. Blue monotony of a cloudless sky; rainless blue June to write by. Visited only by passing planes bringing the unsurprising but welcome news the world still moves beyond these unmoving walls.

Construct meals with a life-raft eye. Go to bed before full dark— though the nocturnal rodents in the roof, along with my reptilian brain, which doesn't trust this place, never let me to go too deep.

Sometimes, in the small hours, I walk outside to piss in the yard. The dog crouches beside me to do the same. Then we sit on the steps a while, beneath the canyon's allotment of night; his chin on my leg, my hand on his head.

The monk Shunryu Suzuki said, *When we were practicing we did not feel anything special. We did not even feel we were leading a monastic life . . . It's the people outside a monastery that feel its atmosphere.*

Here, words filter in. Completing a poem a day is equal parts exhilaration and terror. It's like being on a winning streak in gambling. It's like being in love. The longer it goes on, the more I have to lose when it's over.

For how rarely, if ever, can we not only hear the chants drifting from the monastery windows but follow them inside; then live in that practice until it isn't anything special. Until it's just what is done.

I begin a letter to the poet I cannot finish.

SENT IN THE SUMMER IV

Stieglitz; O'Keeffe
[Between New York and New Mexico]

Stieglitz, July 11:

> . . . Yesterday I wrote you a few desperate letters.
> Forget those letters—forget everything about me except
> those days where you & I were really one—a great
> togetherness.—You gave me back my life—you have
> earned the right to take it . . .

O'Keeffe, July 11:

> . . . when I left New York—it was really with the hope that
> there would be nothing for me—
>
> . . . And now you cry for the center of me that has been
> pushed away for so long—so long—that to tell you the
> truth—I am not sure that it exists anymore—Nobody else
> has ever seen it—or ever will—I seem to meet people here
> with my skin—that doesn't mean anything when I say it—
> but it is the best I can say— . . . the thing you call holy—
> I do not feel any less holy—but I feel more like the rocks
> in the bottom of the stream outside my door—Much
> water runs over me—and I know it—Everyday there
> seems to be more things I am conscious of—and can just
> let pass over me and be—Under it all is something knit to
> you—it will always be that way—I have no choice—you
> have no choice—it just is that way— . . .

BLACK ABSTRACTION

O'Keeffe
[En route to New Mexico; 1930s and '40s]

I.

Days my window-propped elbow
turns shades darker
than the rest of me, I would crush

every passing thing—rust-red silos,
scrub oaks' hardscrabble green,
the mountains blue with distance—

grind it to powder I could cut
with this sky's titanium white
to paint it all whole again.

I've never known you
to make a trip to photograph.
While you men speak of America

yet never travel west
of the Hudson, I want to take the country
in and make it me. Far from New York,

which is brighter by night, I cross
into Texas where dusk ignites
marigold and smolders fast

to bone black. A hard right brings me
to desert. I stop. The air is cold but the car's
bonnet is warm beneath my shoulders.

So dark there is no horizon: all feels
like sky. In such nowhere, my eyes
can hear: the ticking engine, lowing

cattle, loud light of the stars.

II.

The next afternoon, New Mexico.
Trees stoop, the earth reddens, houses
hug the ground, all of it

making the sky ache
with blue. In any view, it is
the focal point—not trees with sky

but sky with everything.

TO FIND YOU III
(GEORGIA O'KEEFFE MUSEUM RESEARCH CENTER)

[Santa Fe, NM; present day, a month earlier]

Just beyond the windows, sprinklers arced steady intervals between trees, which were all in full leaf. It did not feel like desert. The archive's air was cold and dry, its large tables covered in brown leather, topped with brass lamps. Small brown moths fluttered through the room. One landed on my foot.

In low gray rows with small white labels, the drawers were glass-topped, heavy. Regulations required I ask a security guard to pull each out for me, drawer by drawer. He stood above as I knelt and peered.

G1: Source Materials/Animal Bones—Teeth sprouted from a jaw like desert coral, the old bone fissured to woodgrain. Vertebrae like spongiform model airplanes, most no bigger than the moth skating across the glass. So quiet I could hear the fritillation of its wings.

G2: Source Materials/Animal Bones—A photo of O'Keeffe in the back of a car, a fragment of pelvis held to her eye like a monocle. That section of pelvis was in the center of the drawer. A card read, "O'Keeffe used bones to explore the combination of near and far." Propped next to it, a tiny replica of her painting *Pelvis IV*—giant foregrounded pelvis framing a tiny faraway moon.

Outside, a crow plucked grubs from the trunk of a catalpa tree, its leaves broad as a man's palm. They quaked in the breeze. A thousand hallelujah hands flushed through with light.

Box 5—Polaroids, mostly, taken by O'Keeffe, blurred with chemical peel and streak.

Skull and Chair: A cow skull hung on the wall above a straight-backed wooden chair. She had written on the back, "This is at the end of the Portal—beyond the ladder. That chair I paid ninety-eight cents for 22 years ago. One thing I have that is worth its price. It isn't antique. It is from Montgomery Ward. G"

Box 6—Photos of the same chair. She set her paintings in the dirt, propped against its seat, to photograph them for Alfred.

One year of Stieglitz/O'Keeffe original correspondence—1944—in seven ringed archival boxes. Foxed and tea-colored in their acid-free sleeves, I could feel their corners through the plastic.

But three letters were too long, were folded over. The archivist removed them—three sheets of onion skin on the large empty table. She held these. He held these. My breath fluttered their edges. I had the urge to put the corner of one in my mouth. I resisted.

On the page, her "I" whorled like an ear, making the letters so distinctly hers she didn't need to sign them.

The moths stuttered against the white window frame. I noticed her abstract sculpture on the lawn outside—the same lopsided spiral.

How could I care so much for people I'd never met?

PELVIS WITH DISTANCE

O'Keeffe, to Stieglitz
[Abiquiu, NM, to Lake George, NY]

Bone grows from desert
in distance. Bone grows,

girdling sky. Grows
vast and trunkless, sockets

stocked with light. Pelvis
is loupe, is meant

for looking through. Pelvis,
that hollow

and arch.
Distance, basined

by bone, ambit
of absence.

I am, you are,
always

looking
through the other.

IN THE CANYON VIII (FALSE STARTS)

To the poet
[Abiquiu, NM; present day]

Unsent, June 21:

I lose things; do you know that? Wallets, glasses, keys—especially keys. I bring something on the short trip from room to room, mind elsewhere, and lose it completely; then drive myself mad with a frantic search, cursing my tendency toward inattention. Wallets, glasses, keys and now, of course, you. A type of key, I'm sure, though to what I'll likely never know.

Unsent, June 23:

The week you spent in New York took my city and renamed all the streets, designated a new set of landmarks.

13th and 5th: Where you gave me a look that asked, *Is it you? If you are the one, if saving is required, would you, could you do it?*

11th and 6th: The small Jewish cemetery you pointed out, tucked behind a peeling black gate. A street I'd run a hundred times, just like that, made new. Made not just mine but ours.

Unsent, June 24:

Across the lane, the hotel window you leaned out of to throw down your keys.

Unsent, June 27:

The red door. Each time I passed it in the city, I looked left, searching out the stoop on which we sat. Don't be angry, but I have no idea which it is. In memory, there's no distinctive rail or awning. Just the kind of rain more suspended than falling, the kind we didn't really notice beyond a slight prickling on our cheeks—until we looked down and found our clothes soaked through. And you. Hair incandescent against the darkness.

SENT EARLY 1940s

O'Keeffe, to art critic and friend Henry McBride
[Abiquiu, NM, to New York, NY]

I just want to say this to you—You see—I see Alfred as an old man
that I am very fond of—growing older—so that it sometimes
shocks and startles me when he looks pale and tired—Aside from
my fondness for him personally I feel that he has been very
important to something that made my world for me—I like it that
I can make him feel that I have hold of his hand to steady him as
he goes on— . . .

PEDERNAL, 1945

O'Keeffe
[Ghost Ranch, Abiquiu, NM]

The pelvis, sanguine,
buoys an O of atmosphere.
Pedernal's white afterimage

in this bone ship's blue porthole:
oceanous mountains
around a standing wave. Here,

the fulcrum on which sky
rests, the great scale of it—
weighing what, exactly?

What weight loneliness
against all this?

SENT APRIL 18, 7:30 A.M.

O'Keeffe, to Stieglitz
[Telegraph sent while on a train from New York to New Mexico]

I waked once calling you—the faint light from a station made me think your light was on so I called to see if you were alright.

I lay a long time with your letter before I read it.

JULY 13, 1946

O'Keeffe
[New York, NY]

It is difficult on Sundays
in summertime New York.
Heat rains down with nowhere

to go, bounces between buildings,
bringing the air to boil. People, too,
rush from point to point, a daily race

toward stasis. For once, I fall in line.
The roads creep with yellow and black
cars, mine among them. Called east

four days ago, I am ghosted
by desert. All down Madison Avenue,
the long drop to Santa Fe. I watch

the mountains transform—silhouette
stage sets when backlit by sunset,
unreadable palm in the early morning

fog, cupping the city—always there,
though, no matter the changing
light. Past the great museums,

whose walls I coated with a luminous
gray that made each painting float
free of its frame. Alfred understood

such context mattered, how
presentation guides the eye, coaxing
the obdurate mule of the mind.

It was difficult on a Saturday
in summertime New York to find Alfred
a pine coffin. But I did. And stayed

up all night, ripping the seams
of its pink satin interior, relining it
with white linen. I ride beside it

now, a hand on sun-lacquered lid.

SENT JULY 10, 1946

O'Keeffe, final letter to Stieglitz
[Abiquiu, NM, to New York, NY]

It ends:

> My little friend—I don't like to think of you being ill and
> me not there—It bothers me—I hope you are alright by
> now—
>
> A kiss to your funny face~
>
>
> It's a fair clear quiet day—however, Maria tells me it will
> rain—we will see

On the envelope, in another hand:

> found unopened—came too late

IV.

A BLACK BIRD
WITH SNOW-COVERED RED HILLS

O'Keeffe
[Abiquiu, NM; 1949]

After years shared at a distance,
I am already accustomed

to an empty bed. I summon
the dogs from the morning

melt, their garland of red prints
mudding the floors. Walls

breathe back the stove's heat.
As long as I am here, you can still be

in New York, grousing
about your bowels and feet.

I pull on overshoes, walk, sketch.
You lunch with old friends

at the gallery. I make dinner.
Read. Wear your sweater to bed,

the blue one. Fall asleep writing to you
in my head, of that day, the next,

knees tucked so tight to my chest
I hold my own soles, Cannon-ball!

through the night. And you
are there, taking sun on the dock,

sputtering as my lake-splash
startles you awake. Love,

come join me in this water.

THE WHITE PLACE IN SHADOW

O'Keeffe
[Plaza Blanca, NM; 1949]

I paint them in such
close-up—spires
in high desert, sandstone
coated by white lava
ash—a viewer cannot know
that central darkness
means the sun is setting

the clouds on fire, or how
an arroyo wraps this
formation like a moat,
red walls carved smooth
by seasonal flooding,
which leaves the wash
littered with carcasses.
How strange

it must be to drown
in the desert. Earlier,
when noon slayed all
the shadows, I lay in it,
the only sound

occasional bird cries.

IN THE CANYON IX (LONELINESS)

[Abiquiu, NM; present day]

Tho we all strive to be free, freedom can be very lonely.
— O'Keeffe

I can't sleep, so read by headlamp until beetles bounce off the page
and palm-sized moths scribble dry wings across my eyes.

My mother, married to my father for thirty-nine years and
counting, says, *I never thought of marriage as forever. Otherwise I couldn't
have said yes.*

> No one as perfect for her as she is for herself; down in her
> craft room, audiobook occupying just enough surface to
> let her deeper mind go about its underground business; her
> hands busy binding glass shards with copper, mosaicking
> old frames.

Always making something broken whole; something old,
new. Always the one who most appreciates
these transformations.
Yet sleeping each night
in my father's strong arms.

When O'Keeffe painted her *Music* series (abstractions of deep
pools and petals, music "translated into something for the eye"),
Stieglitz created *Music: A Sequence of Ten Cloud Photographs* (light-
limned puffs of cumulus; cirrostratus like a threadbare blanket
hung out to dry)—

a kind of artistic call-and-response,
a love lyric enough to hang on gallery walls.

Yet all those months apart, all those letters of
longing and recrimination.

Loneliness of one kind or loneliness of another.
Can one person possibly act as balm for them all?

The dog whines. I sit up and pet him. Stop. Begin again, unable to
believe: With each pass of my hand, a stripe of bioluminescent
beads rolls down his side: *Pet. Glow. Pet. Glow.*

Astonishing. But who else is here to witness?

An unshared life is only
half-lived,
unetched by mutual memory.

IN THE PATIO IV (BLACK DOOR)

O'Keeffe
[Abiquiu House Courtyard; 1950]

Carried inside me
long as I can remember,
a child's drawing of a door:

four lines, none plumb,
pressed into an adobe wall
of thumb-smudged pink.

Now here—after how many
years of rendering interior
exterior so that others

might see—
the world has made one
for me. A door

is everything a painting
wants to be. Portal, promise.
I was afraid it was perfect

only so long as I did not
enter it. But in the painting
I do not paint, I lie, knees propped

to either side of the jamb,
sill bisecting me right
as a spine—each crack

vertebra matched: perfectly
in, perfectly out—
to both worlds, peripheral.

SENT AUGUST 4, 1950

O'Keeffe, to Stieglitz's nephew William Howard Schubart
[Abiquiu, NM, to Lake George, NY]

It seems odd to think of you at Lake George tonight . . .

. . . I will never go back there—unless—maybe to stand just for a
moment where I put the little bit that was left of Alfred after he
was cremated—But I think not even for that.

I put him where he would hear the Lake—

That is finished.

. . . Good night to you at Lake George—

G.

I am glad I am not there.

IN THE PATIO VIII (GREEN DOOR)

O'Keeffe [Abiquiu, NM; 1950]

When I stand alone with the earth and sky a feeling of something in me going off in every direction into the unknown of infinity means more to me than anything any organized religion gives me.—O'Keeffe

Every day this week
feels like Sunday.
From the roof,

I listen to Easter
until earth
and wall slip

their skins,
become one
ceaseless

russet—dirt,
brick—in thrall
to the maw

of a late-day
shadow, the door
half-devoured.

Buckshot of clouds.
Church processions
framed by black

mesa. Singing
so loud the hills'
echoes sing back.

Remnant of an old
faith. I go inside
to make mint tea.

IN THE CANYON X
(UNCOVERING THE MIRRORS)

[Abiquiu, NM; present day]

I fast, go on a long hike. Flip through Barthes' *Camera Lucida*, read,
I know better a photograph that I remember
than one I am looking at.

At the end of the day, beyond tiredness, beyond hunger, I go to the
wall beside my bed and uncover the large mirror.
For a moment, two distinct overlays:
a flash of first impression, as though after a month away I'm
seeing myself as another might upon meeting me for the first time;

the second, an instant of what I've sensed but not seen: a strong
face, a not just good but a best day face.

Georgia, I came here thinking you'd teach me how to be alone. That
if I uncovered your secret, I could reverse-engineer a life by what
I'd learned.

But now I suspect you could leave your
known world behind because you knew you were loved—however
imperfectly.
Because Alfred was a home you could always return to.

I finish my letter to the poet
and set it on the sill. Promise myself I'll mail it
—though I'm not sure I will.

TO FIND YOU IV
(O'KEEFFE'S ABIQUIU HOUSE)

[Abiquiu, NM; present day, a month earlier]

Bushes of mulberry, rosemary, cherry;
trees of filbert, plum, and peach—all
useful. Beside the ladder leading
to the roof, blue and yellow columbine,
head-high stalk of hollyhock, unblossomed
buds like pursed green stars.

In the back, the view unobstructed
was somehow less than the same view
framed by your studio window.

A bush of the sage that ranges
ragged across these basins was,
in your patio, trimmed like bonsai,
tame as a housecat. How did you see

into this once-ruin of adobe
and mud, used by villagers as a sty
for their pigs, and know—both the vision
of what it could be and that your will
could make it so?

You hired local women
to daub and smooth; every surface
leveled by a woman's hands. I stood
in the shadow of your patio door,
breathing its coat of acrid shellac,
dust eddying up in the afternoon light.

COMPOSITE [SELF-]PORTRAIT
AS WISE DESERT ELDER

O'Keeffe
[Abiquiu, NM; 1976]

I was 32, and she was 79 . . . I took some pictures . . . [then
the] game had ended, and I'd won.
                              —Photographer John Loengard

All these men
with cameras
in hand,
comparing the length
of their lenses.
I am not twenty-nine

anymore. I am no one's
wife. I own
and abide in two
houses and inhabit
my face as fully.
In my desert,

I orchestrate
the light, seat
myself beneath
this cow skull.
I need them only
to take the picture.

SENT AUGUST

O'Keeffe, to curator Carl Zigrosser
[Abiquiu, NM, to New York, NY]

I was the last person shown at 291—you might for my benefit put
in a sentence to the effect that [Stieglitz] did not know me personally
when he gave me the 2 shows at 291—

It often sounds as if I was born and taught to walk by him—and
never thought of painting till he worked on me—I don't really care
but I know I've had to be both strong and tough to survive—on
second thought—I suppose whether he knew me or not at that
time has nothing to do with this thing you are doing—so if you
leave it out I don't care—such things matter so little in the long
run— . . .

GEORGIA O'KEEFFE, BY ALFRED STIEGLITZ (COMPOSITE PORTRAIT)

O'Keeffe
[While compiling Stieglitz's early portraits of her into a book, Abiquiu, NM; 1978]

When I look over the photographs Stieglitz took of me—some of them more than sixty years ago—I wonder who that person is. It is as if in my one life I have lived many lives.—O'Keeffe

Tilted black bowler,
white collar just so:
androgynous dandy,
fingers splayed
as any mouth
in amateur soft-core.

It was so much easier
to just disappear. One grows
tired of insisting.

Cowled scowler, arched
brow; propped against
a wooden wall, stuck
with hay and staples.

When we were just words,
I mailed him hasty bundles
of brown wrap and twine.
He shellacked my drawings
with fixative, chided me
a careless mother. But
the instant I gave them

to another's eyes—even
his—they were no longer mine.

These portrait selves, the same.

Unheaded torso against
diaphanous screen,
pelvic jut and breast,
muscled chest, dark
rivers of thigh.

Public carapace, a surprising
relief. Aquifer-me freed
to branch subterranean.
While, overhead, the clicking
whisper of his acquisitive eye.

IN THE CANYON XI (TO THE POET)

[Abiquiu, NM; June 30, present day]

This cabin, I've learned, was conceived as a line camp, a way-station for cowboys pushing cattle up or down the western mesa. Construction began late summer, a group of men hired in town to build it—Mexican fieldhands and one lone gringo, barely in his twenties, working his way west, seeking something the college he'd dropped out of hadn't given him. So he worked this land for a season; clearing roads, stretching miles of barbed wire around posts he'd hewn and planted, helping build this place. And all the while falling for the ranch-owner overseeing him, a woman whose home had earthen floors that required daily watering; who had no electricity, but a grand piano.

By the time they put on the roof, it was winter. As the crew fitted tarps atop the rafters, piled on insulating dirt, and covered it with tin, she sat on the cold ground cooking rice for the men, warmed by the fact she'd fallen right back for this boy eighteen years younger than her youngest son, this good man who stood on the roof, throwing down kisses to her in the snow.

After they married, their first Christmas was spent in this cabin. The silver bulbs they hung from the juniper off the porch still sway and shine as I write this, twenty years on.

From a branch there, a goldfinch bobs and weaves, stitching a bright yellow seam through the blue. The sage silvers in the sun and the wind hawks across the porch, hovering the rugs. Which is all to say I'm writing to you from a sacred space, from a monument to improbable love. I imagine you here with me, lying on the worn wood of this bench—the sharp cross-bedding of your shoulder blades, the twinned arroyos tracing your spine. The fine down on your lower back sending up small flares into the afternoon light. My mouth on your sun-warm skin.

Which is to say I am still in love with you.

Terrifying as it is to offer this so nakedly—to risk the chance you find it, find me, lacking—after so many years without you, I'm far more frightened of a life in which I didn't have the courage to offer, the courage to ask.

You are the only home I've ever known.

SKY ABOVE CLOUDS IV

O'Keeffe
[Ghost Ranch, Abiquiu, NM;1978]

There were other things I meant
to paint. There a river; there
a road. Here, the sky below.

For that painting, my 77th summer—
twenty-four feet of canvas
stretched taut as a sail. I painted

all day, mixing vats of a single color.
Each evening, I walked into sunset,
wind rippling the sage, which lapped

at my waist, launching sprays
of swallowtails and speckled
grasshoppers, orange wings flaring

from their rough-barked flanks.
A quarter-mile out, I turned, and there,
amid bricks of red earth, in the open

bay of the garage: my painting
of the sky from a plane. Clouds
like a path of flat-topped stones

from one bank of a stream
to the other. It cast
its cool light along the ground,

a light I created. In the Shelton,
—do you remember?—
who could say we were not gods,

of that moment, at least—
as we stood naked before the high
window. My back to your chest. A draft

stippling our skin as we looked out
over the gaslit tumult of our city,
watching snow fall down away from us.

ONCE IN HER EIGHTIES
GEORGIA ATTEMPTS A JOKE

O'Keeffe
[Abiquiu, NM; 1978]

Sex is not flowers. Death
is not bones. Loneliness is
not desert. I am not
my paintings.

Wait, let me try
again.

My flowers are not sex.
My bones are not death.

All those critics, their
honorifics: "Priestess
of Eternal Woman,"
"Lady of the Lilies."
They make me

seem unearthly, feeding
on air; when, truth is, I like
beef steak—and I like it rare.

TO FIND YOU V (QUESTIONS FOR GEORGIA)

I was six when you died.

Is that why it's so hard to see you
as anything but outside
of time?

Did you ever water ski on Abiquiu Lake?
Watch the moon landing?
Drink Tang?
Listen to the Beatles,
Velvet Underground,
Joni Mitchell?
Did you own a pair of Converse?
Wear something lacy,
even once,
under that chambray shirt?
Did you use a computer?
Rollerskate?
Worry about your karma or your chi?

Would you have liked me?

LIKE AN EARLY BLUE ABSTRACTION

O'Keeffe
[Abiquiu, NM; 1979]

*By the time O'Keeffe did these watercolors in the mid-to-late
1970s, she had lost all but her peripheral vision. . . . She chose
brushes by feel*
.—Jill Krementz

Dawn and dusk, the same path—foot-worn,
pebble-strewn, soft rustle of wind

in the ricegrass. This is my country,
so it little matters I can no longer see it.

Roll a sprig of sage between fingertips. Inhale.
That is all I need to know of green.

Seeing left me from the center out. To even glimpse
a thing I must look away from it,

unshackle my focus, let it find its way in
to the periphery. The dogs trail behind—

scrabble of nails in soil, rank breath
on my heels. If they're gone, it's to find me

something—a length of leg bone, daisy-chain
of vertebrae. I let my hands take them in:

shin's long notch along the side,
tipped with a four-grooved joint, beveled

like the head of a fine violin. Backbone
is a festival of flat and arch—sharp-lipped

fins feel made for flying; between each
ridge, fibrous gristle of cartilage. Rasp

of dog tongue on my fingertips. Sink
of patted fur. Then they sidle aside.

IN THE CANYON XII (LAST RUN)

[Abiquiu, NM; present day]

The caretaker will arrive soon with his truck. My gear is packed, the poet's letter stowed in my bag.

My last run here begins slowly, but the dog is having none of it. He races into the riverbed around the first bend. My legs respond, strong from a month of sand-sunk miles.

Our tracks are everywhere, crisscrossed by streamers from snake bellies, the arrow fletching of finch prints.

I run and listen to the near no-sound of my feet in the sand. Close my eyes for long stretches to feel each step's mash and rasp, the clean dry air, the morning sun.

This is what I do, this is just what is done.

A part of me is disappointed the hallucinations never came, as though the canyon were a drug that hadn't quite kicked in. But instead of hearing things not there, perhaps it is enough to have heard more of what was.

MAY 6, 1986

Later the bells will ring from St. Thomas,
peal down from Abiquiu across the Chama

into the valley warming with spring; sound
in the trumpets of the jimson blossoms

unfurling for evening, along sun-flushed
cliffs gone to brick with last light,

moon-glown elk bones just freed
from thaw, endless hills of juniper,

pine. Later they will ring from the old
adobe church; but, for now, Georgia

is at her window. *The canvas
is so much larger now, and I am*

no longer separated from it by brushes.
She paints herself a door and walks through.

SELECTED BIBLIOGRAPHY

Regarding O'Keeffe and Stieglitz:

Barthes, Roland. *Camera Lucida: Reflections on Photography.* Trans. Richard Howard. Foreword by Geoff Dyer. New York: Hill and Wang, 2010.

Benke, Britta. *O'Keeffe.* Koln: Taschen, 1995.

Cowart, Jack, Juan Hamilton, and Sarah Greenough. *Georgia O'Keeffe: Art and Letters.* [exh. cat. National Gallery of Art, Washington]. Boston: New York Graphic Society Books, 1987.

Drohojowska-Philp, Hunter. *Full Bloom: The Art and Life of Georgia O'Keeffe.* New York: W.W. Norton & Company Inc., 1995.

Georgia O'Keeffe: A Life in Art. Dir. Perry Miller Adato. The Georgia O'Keeffe Museum, 2003.

Giboire, Clive, ed. Lovingly, *Georgia: The Complete Correspondence of Georgia O'Keeffe and Anita Pollitzer.* New York: Simon & Schuster, 1990.

Heilbrun, Françoise, ed. *Alfred Stieglitz (1864-1946).* Paris: Musée d'Orsay, 2004.

The J. Paul Getty Museum. *In Focus: Alfred Stieglitz: Photographs from the J. Paul Getty Museum.* Naef, Weston, ed. Malibu: The J. Paul Getty Museum, 1995.

Lisle, Laurie. *Portrait of an Artist: A Biography of Georgia O'Keeffe.* New York: Seaview Books, 1980. Rev. ed., New York: Washington Square Press, 1987.

Loengard, John. *Georgia O'Keeffe: At Ghost Ranch.* New York: Stewart, Tabori, and Chang, 1995.

O'Keeffe, Georgia. *Georgia O'Keeffe.* New York: Viking Press, 1976. Reprint, New York: Penguin Books, 1985.

——. *Some Memories of Drawings.* New York: Viking Press, 1976.

——. *Introduction to Georgia O'Keeffe: A Portrait by Alfred Stieglitz.* [exh. cat., The Metropolitan Museum of Art, New York]. New York, 1978.

—— and Alfred Stieglitz. *My Faraway One: Selected Letters of Georgia O'Keeffe and Alfred Stieglitz: Volume One, 1915-1933.* Ed. Sarah

Greenough. New Haven: Yale University Press, 2011.

Robinson, Roxana. *Georgia O'Keeffe: A Life.* Lebanon: University Press of New England, 1989.

Solnit, Rebecca. *River of Shadows: Edweard Muybridge and the Technological Wild West.* New York: Penguin, 2003.

Sontag, Susan. *On Photography.* New York: Farrar, Strauss, and Giroux, 1977.

Wagner, Anne Middleton. *Three Artists (Three Women): Modernism and the Art of Hesse, Krasner, and O'Keeffe.* Berkeley, Los Angeles: University of California Press, 1996.

Regarding the "In the Canyon" and "To Find You" sequences:

Cooper, David A. *God is a Verb: Kabbalah and the Practice of Mystical Judaism.* New York: Riverhead Books, 1998.

Derrida, Jacques. *Archive Fever: A Freudian Impression.* Trans. Eric Prenowitz.Chicago: University of Chicago Press, 1998.

Lopez, Barry. *Desert Notes.* New York: Avon Books, 1976.

Solnit, Rebecca. *A Field Guide to Getting Lost.* New York: Penguin, 2005.

Suzuki, Shunryu. *Zen Mind, Beginner's Mind: Informal Talks on Zen Meditation and Practice.* Boston: Weatherhill, 1999.

NOTES

13, Epigraphs
O'Keeffe's quote is taken from *O'Keeffe* by Georgia O'Keeffe (accompanying illustration I, Blue Lines, n.p.); Lopez's quote is from the introduction to *Desert Notes* (xii).

15, In the Canyon I (Arrival)
In June 2012, I lived alone in a primitive cabin tucked away in a canyon in Abiquiu, NM, the area in which O'Keeffe spent the final thirty years of her life. The majority of these poems were written there.

I.

19, Red Barn in Wheatfield
Painting: O'Keeffe Museum, Accession No. 1997.06.25
Born in 1887, O'Keeffe spent her childhood in rural Sun Prairie, WI, with four sisters and two brothers. She thought of herself as an artist from an early age and wrote she had always had "things in my head that are not like what anyone has taught me—shapes and ideas so near to me" (O'Keeffe *O'Keeffe* accompanying illustration I, Blue Lines, n.p.).

21, Alfred Stieglitz at 291 (First Encounter)
Photograph: Metropolitan Museum of Art, Accession No. 33.43.29
One of the most innovative and famous photographers of the twentieth century, Alfred Stieglitz also ran New York City galleries instrumental in introducing to the U.S. many of the premiere avant-garde European artists of his day, giving artists including Brancusi, Duchamp, Matisse, and Picasso their first American shows.

While studying at the conservative Art Students League, O'Keeffe and her classmates visited Stieglitz's gallery to see what their

117

instructors considered a "controversial" exhibit of drawings by the sculptor Auguste Rodin. O'Keeffe found her first encounter with Stieglitz intimidating, and wrote, "I very well remember the fantastic violence of Stieglitz's defense when the students with me began talking with him about the drawings. I had never heard anything like it, so I went into the farthest corner and waited for the storm to be over" (Lisle 47-48). She was twenty-one; he, forty-five and married, with a young daughter.

23, Untitled (Dead Rabbit with Copper Pot)
Painting: Art Students League of New York, Control No. IAP 82380053.
O'Keeffe was trained in the classical style, which valued imitation over innovation. While studying at the Art Students League, she won a top prize for her painting of a rabbit, rendered in a style similar to that of her instructor William Merritt Chase. Outside influences are also apparent in the works described in the poem, *"Untitled (Arm)" and "Untitled (West Lawn of University of Virginia)."*

24, Sent August 14, 1915
O'Keeffe wrote this while teaching summer school at the University of Virginia (*My Faraway One* 3).

25, Early Abstraction
Drawing: Milwaukee Art Museum Accession No. M1997.189
While teaching in South Carolina, O'Keeffe wrote, "It was in the fall of 1915 that I first had the idea that what I had been taught was of little value to me except for the use of my materials as a language . . . I decided to start anew—to strip away what I had been taught—to accept as true my own thinking. This was one of the best times of my life" (O'Keeffe *O'Keeffe* accompanying illustration 1, *Blue Lines,* n.p.).

In a letter to Stieglitz on February 1, 1916, she wrote, ". . . Words and I—are not good friends at all except with some people—when I'm close to them and can feel as well as hear their response—I have to say it some way—Last year I went color mad—but I've almost hated to think of color since the fall went—I've been slaving on the violin—trying to make that talk—I wish I could tell you some of the things I've wanted to say as I've felt them" (*My Faraway One* 4).

26, No. 8—Special (Palo Duro Canyon with Spiral)
Painting: Whitney Museum of Art Accession No. 85.52
After her time in South Carolina, O'Keeffe taught at the West Texas State Normal College in Canyon, TX. Venturing into the nearby Palo Duro Canyon with her sister, O'Keeffe wrote they "sometimes had to go down together holding to a horizontal stick to keep one another from falling. . . Those perilous climbs were frightening but it was wonderful to me and not like anything I had known before" (O'Keeffe *O'Keeffe* accompanying illustration 5, Painting No. 21, n.p.). Though many of the paintings inspired by Texas were painted after her return to New York, the sounds of Canyon were still with her. "The cattle in the pens lowing for their calves day and night was a sound that had always haunted me," she wrote. "It had a regular rhythmic beat like the old Penitente songs, repeating the same rhythms over and over all through the day and night. It was loud and raw under the stars in that wide empty country" (O'Keeffe *O'Keeffe* accompanying illustration 3, From the Plains, n.p.).

27, In the Canyon II (Fear/Breaking)
The discussion of the different types of *tikkun* is from the midrash of Rabbi Isaac Luria, as discussed in *God is a Verb* by Rabbi David A. Cooper.

29, To Find You (Georgia O'Keeffe Museum)
References the show "Georgia O'Keeffe and the Faraway: Nature and Image," which ran May 11, 2012 to May 5, 2013. O'Keeffe's quote is from the documentary film *Georgia O'Keeffe: A Life in Art.*

31, Coney Island, 1917
After being escorted from Canyon, TX, to New York by the pho-
tographer Paul Strand at Stieglitz's behest, O'Keeffe met up with
Stieglitz for the second time. On June 20, 1917, O'Keeffe wrote to
her friend Anita Pollitzer about a trip to Coney Island with Alfred
Stieglitz for Decoration Day (now known as Memorial Day). She
wrote only, "It was a great party and a great day—" (Cowart 163).

33, Sent June 6, 1917
One of a long series of letters written by Stieglitz in an attempt to
persuade O'Keeffe to return to New York (*My Faraway One* 157).

34, Nude Series VIII
Painting: Georgia O'Keeffe Museum No. 1997.04.11
In 1917, O'Keeffe painted her only extant self-portraits. During
this time, her exchange with Stieglitz grew more charged. In July,
she wrote, "I undressed—painted again on myself—I guess that
excited me—my head full of wheels again" (*My Faraway One* 176).

Earlier in their correspondence she had written, "I put this in an enve-
lope—stretched—and laughed—/It's so funny that I should just
write you because I want to—I wonder if many people do.—/You
see—I would go in and talk to you if I could—and I hate to be com-
pletely outdone by a little thing like distance—" (*My Faraway One* 5).

35, Music—Pink and Blue II
Painting: Whitney Museum of Art, Accession No. 91.90
In 1918, Stieglitz cobbled together enough financial support for
O'Keeffe to quit her teaching job in Texas and move to New York
for a year to paint. She moved into his niece Elizabeth's studio and,
though he was still married, Stieglitz almost immediately moved
into the studio with her. Painted in that first year of living with
Stieglitz, the "Music" series strove to translate music into "some-
thing for the eye" (O'Keeffe *O'Keeffe* accompanying illustration 14,
Music—Pink and Blue I, 1919, n.p.).

Later, on May 16, 1922, O'Keeffe wrote to Stieglitz from York Beach, ME, "It even seems to be my only memory of you—two bodies that have fused—have touched with completeness at both ends making a complete circuit . . . The circle with two centers— each touching the other . . ." (*My Faraway One* 368).

36, In the Canyon III (Love)
The letter from O'Keeffe to Millay is quoted in Nancy Milford's *Savage Beauty: The Life of Edna St. Vincent Millay* (341).

II.

39, To Find You II (On Stieglitz's Photos of O'Keeffe)
Throughout their life together, Stieglitz took over 300 portraits of O'Keeffe, an astonishing number for that time.

40, Self-Portrait in Absentia
Photograph: "*Georgia O'Keeffe*," *Metropolitan Museum of Art, Accession No. 1997.61.22*
The first epigraph is from O'Keeffe's introduction to *Georgia O'Keeffe: A Portrait by Alfred Stieglitz*. Thanks for many of the observations in this poem go to Anne Middleton Wagner's analysis of this image in her brilliant book *Three Artists (Three Women): Modernism and the Art of Hesse, Krasner, and O'Keeffe* (93-95).

42, Georgia O'Keeffe (Half-Naked, in White)
Photograph: Metropolitan Museum of Art, Accession No. 1997.61.54
Stieglitz's early photos of O'Keeffe—erotic, many of them nudes—shaped much of the critical and public perception of her work for decades to come, sexualized and sexist perceptions she resented and pushed back against.

44, Plate 28 (Clothed in Only a Swim Cap)
Photograph: J. Paul Getty Museum, In Focus: Alfred Stieglitz (62)

47, Lake George, 1922
Painting: San Francisco Museum of Art, Accession No. 52.6714
Stieglitz's family had a home in Lake George, NY. At first,
O'Keeffe viewed the house as a retreat; later, as a crowded incon-
venience that impinged on her time to paint.

48, Alfred Faces the Camera, Georgia Turns Away
*Photograph: "Alfred Stieglitz and Georgia O'Keeffe, New York City" Alfred
Newman, 1944; Howard Greenberg Gallery*
A brief account of their wedding is given in *Full Bloom: The Art and
Life of Georgia O'Keeffe* (Drohojowska-Philip 241-242). Though
they were married for twenty-two years, O'Keeffe kept her own
name, saying, "I had a hard time hanging onto it, but I wasn't going
to give it up. Why should I take someone else's famous name? So
when people would say 'Mrs. Stieglitz,' I would say 'Miss
O'Keeffe'" (Dorothy Seiberling, "Horizons of a Pioneer," *Life*,
March 1, 1968, p. 52).

50, Sent 1926
(Cowart *Georgia O'Keeffe* 183)

51, The Shelton with Sunspots
Painting: Art Institute of Chicago, Accession No. 1985.206
In 1976, O'Keeffe wrote, "I painted 'The Shelton with Sunspots'
in 1926. I went out one morning to look at it before I started to
work and there was the optical illusion of a bite out of one side of
the tower made by the sun, with sunspots against the building and
against the sky. I made that painting beginning at the upper left
and went off at the lower right without going back" (O'Keeffe *Some
Memories* n.p.).

53, Wave, Night
Painting: Addison Gallery of American Art, Accession No. 1947.33
In August 1926, troubled by Stieglitz' flirtation and possible
infidelities with several young women at Lake George, O'Keeffe

left to stay with friends in York Beach, ME. They continued to write and, "concerned that there was 'a black ugly wall' between them," Stieglitz went to York Beach, where he and O'Keeffe discovered a "newfound sense of love and commitment" (*My Faraway One* 368).

54, An American Place Exhibition Catalogue (The Flower Paintings)
The text in plain font was written by O'Keeffe for the exhibition catalogue "Georgia O'Keeffe," a show at An American Place, January 22-March 17, 1939 (Archives of American Art, Whitney Museum Papers, roll N679, frame 168). She painted the majority of her flower paintings in the 1920s, in an attempt to create work to which sexual interpretations could not apply. This strategy backfired; the magnified flowers were touted as erotic masterpieces.

III.

59, Sent in the Summer I
(*My Faraway One* 429-442)
After first visiting New Mexico in 1929 as the guest of Mabel Dodge Luhan, O'Keeffe began to regularly spend her summers in New Mexico. While this time marked a period of intense productivity for her, these extended absences placed a great strain on her relationship with Stieglitz.

During her initial visits, O'Keeffe first painted close views of objects like trees, as though not quite ready to open herself to the overwhelming expanse of the high desert landscape.

61, From the Faraway, Nearby
Painting: Metropolitan Museum of Art, Accession Number 59.204.12
Marsden Hartley, the painter, poet, and essayist, wrote to Stieglitz of his visit to New Mexico, "This country is very beautiful and also difficult . . . it is not a country of light on things. It is a coun-

try of things in light, therefore is a country of form, with a new presentation of light as problem," (Charles Eldredge, Julie Schimmel, and William Truettner, *Art in New Mexico*. New York: Abbeville, 1986. P. 333).

62, In the Canyon VI (Hallucinations)
The epigraph of the quote by Susan Stewart is via the artist/maker Ann Hamilton, speaking with Krista Tippett for the radio show "On Being" ("Ann Hamilton—Making, and the Spaces We Share," February 13, 2014).

64, Sent in the Summer II
(*My Faraway One* 451-452), Letter to Paul Strand (Cowart 190)
The fact that O'Keeffe not only bought a car on her own but kept that fact from her husband for over a month was an anomaly for this time, representing her extreme independence.

65, The Grey Hills
Painting: Indianapolis Museum of Art No. 898 10746
O'Keeffe wrote and spoke often of using her car as a traveling studio. The anecdote about the bees is adapted from an extended reminiscence about her visits to the Black Place when she had to choose between wilting in the heat of her closed car and getting stung by inquisitive bees (O'Keeffe *O'Keeffe*, accompanying illustration 59, *Grey Hills II*, n.p.).

67, Sent in the Summer III
(*My Faraway One* 452-462)
While Stieglitz was pleading with O'Keeffe to return and pressuring her with threats of suicide, he was embarking on an affair with Dorothy Norman, a woman in her mid-twenties, forty-one years his junior. Of their relatively open marriage, O'Keeffe wrote to Stieglitz in 1934, "The difference in us is that when I felt myself attracted to some one else I realized I must make a choice—and I made it in your favor. . . . You seemed to feel there was no need to

make a choice" (Collection of O'Keeffe Museum Research Center).

68, Road to Pedernal
Painting: O'Keeffe Museum, Accession No. 2006.05.170
Pedernal Mountain was visible from O'Keeffe's Ghost Ranch home. Of it, she often joked, "It belongs to me. God told me if I painted it often enough, I could have it" (Lisle 295).

72, Sent in the Summer IV
(*My Faraway One* 471-473)
During this time, Stieglitz begins to use her name more in letters than he has before, as though trying to summon her, to tell her that he sees her and can name her and therefore she is his.

73, Black Abstraction
Painting: Metropolitan Museum of Art, Accession Number 69.278.2
O'Keeffe said she based this painting on a vision she had after waking from anesthesia. Yet, the pinprick of haloed light against a black backdrop has always reminded me the headlights of a car on one of the many dark lonely roads in the southwest.

77, Pelvis with Distance
Painting: Indianapolis Museum of Art, Accession No. 77.229
In the exhibition catalogue for her 1944 show, O'Keeffe wrote, ". . . when I started painting the pelvis bones I was most interested in the holes in the bones—what I saw through them—particularly the blue from holding them up in the sun against the sky as one is apt to do when one seems to have more sky than earth in one's world . . . they were most beautiful against the Blue—that Blue that will always be there as it is now after all man's destruction is finished" (O'Keeffe *O'Keeffe*, accompanying illustration 74, *Pelvis III*, n.p.).

80, Sent Early 1940s
(Cowart 244)

81, Pedernal, 1945
Painting: O'Keeffe Museum, Accession No. 1977.06.08
In the circle of blue above the mountain in this painting, there is
the faint chalked outline of Pedernal Mountain, visible only when
seeing the painting in person.

82, Sent April 18, 7:30 a.m.
From the archives of the Georgia O'Keeffe Museum Research
Center.

83, July 13, 1946
Photograph: ["Georgia O'Keeffe"], Metropolitan Museum of Art, Accession No.
N.A.2005.17
O'Keeffe was in Abiquiu when Stieglitz suffered a stroke on
Wednesday, July 10, 1946. She arrived in New York to find him in
the coma in which he remained until his death early Saturday
morning, July 13, 1946 (Lisle 335-336).

85, Sent July 10, 1946
Letter and envelope held in the Alfred Stieglitz/Georgia O'Keeffe
Archive of Yale University's Beinecke Rare Book & Manuscript
Library.

IV.

89, A Black Bird with Snow-Covered Red Hills
Painting: Anonymous Collection, Control No. 898.10840
About this painting, O'Keeffe wrote, "One morning the world was
covered in snow. It became another painting . . . a black bird flying,
always there, always going away." (O'Keeffe *O'Keeffe* accompanying
illustration for *A Black Bird with Snow-Covered Red Hills*, n.p.).
O'Keeffe biographer Hunter Drohojowska-Philp called this painting
a "hidden portrait of Stieglitz," speculating that the stylized crow
soaring above the hills alluded to one of O'Keeffe's nicknames for
Stieglitz, "Old Crow Feather" (419).

91, The White Place in Shadow
Painting: Anonymous Collection, San Francisco, CA, Accession No. IAP 89810749
O'Keeffe first began painting what she referred to as "The White Place" on a camping trip there in 1940. After Stieglitz's death, she was reticent in sharing her grief and in response to most expressions of sympathy she "merely acknowledged that it was a time of change for her, that she was learning to be alone in a new way" (Lisle 337).

92, In the Canyon IX (Loneliness)
The epigraph by O'Keeffe is from a note written in 1981 to Juan Hamilton, her friend and assistant (Collection of O'Keeffe Museum Research Center).

Dropping in on a class at Teachers College, Columbia University, O'Keeffe saw Alon Bement instruct his students to interpret music through charcoal drawings. She said, "This gave me an idea that I was very interested to follow later—the idea that music could be translated into something for the eye, the idea of lines like sounds," (O'Keeffe *O'Keeffe* accompanying illustration 14, *Music—Pink and Blue I, 1919*, n.p.).

94, In the Patio IV (Black Door)
Painting: Museum of Fine Arts, Accession No. 1990.434
Though O'Keeffe already owned a home at Ghost Ranch, she had an eye out for a second home in which she could grow her own fruits and vegetables. About her first trip to what eventually became her Abiquiu House, she wrote, "As I climbed and walked about in the ruin I found a patio . . . with a long door on one side. That wall with a door in it was something I had to have. It took me ten years to get it—three more years to fix the house so I could live in it—and after that the wall with a door was painted many times" (O'Keeffe O'Keeffe accompanying illustration 82, *Patio with Black Door, 1955*, n.p.).

95, Sent August 4, 1950

William Howard Schubart, one of Stieglitz's nephews, managed O'Keeffe's finances for several years (Cowart 254).

96, In the Patio VIII (Green Door)

Painting: Georgia O'Keeffe Museum IAP 89810855

The O'Keeffe epigraph is from a letter to William Howard Schubart, July 25, 1952 (Cowart 263). O'Keeffe describes listening to the weeklong Easter celebration in a letter to William Howard Schubart on April 6, 1950 (Cowart 251).

98, In the Canyon X (Uncovering the Mirrors)

(Barthes 53).

100, Composite [Self-]Portrait as Wise Desert Elder

Examples of later photographs: "Georgia O'Keeffe on Her Roof," John Loengard; "Georgia O'Keeffe," Yousuf Karsh, Metropolitan Museum of Art, Accession No. 67.543.38, "Georgia O'Keeffe, Ghost Ranch, New Mexico," Arnold Newman

The epigraph is from John Loengard's *Georgia O'Keeffe: At Ghost Ranch* (5-7).

101, Sent August

Compared to the letter "Sent 1926" in which she wrote, "I feel like a little plant that he has watered and weeded and dug around—" (p. 50 in this book), I love how this letter shows O'Keeffe's evolution from star-struck neophyte to self-assured artist, confident enough in her own abilities that she can ultimately disregard others' beliefs about Stieglitz's role in her success (Cowart 236).

102, Georgia O'Keeffe by Alfred Stieglitz (Composite Portrait)

Photographs: Androgynous dandy: "Georgia O'Keeffe," Metropolitan Museum of Art, Accession No. 1997.61.4; Cowled scowler: "Georgia O'Keeffe," Metropolitan Museum of Art, Accession No. 1997.61.24; Torso: "Georgia O'Keeffe—Torso," Metropolitan Museum of Art, Accession No. 28.130.2

The epigraph is from O'Keeffe's introduction to her curation of

Stieglitz's portraits of her, *Georgia O'Keeffe: A Portrait by Alfred Stieglitz.* She went on to write, "His idea of a portrait was not just one picture. His dream was to start with a child at birth . . . As a portrait it would be a photographic diary."

106, Sky Above Clouds IV
Painting: Art Institute of Chicago, Accession No. 1983.821
About her paintings of the Radiator Building in New York, she wrote, "When you live up high, the snow and rain go down and away from you instead of coming toward you from above. I was never able to do anything with that. There were many other things I meant to paint. I still see them when I am in the Big City" (O'Keeffe *O'Keeffe* accompanying illustration 20, *Radiator-Building— Night, New York,* n.p.).

108, Once in Her Eighties Georgia Attempts a Joke
O'Keeffe was frequently displeased with critics, who often applied Freudian interpretations and reductively emphasized her work as an expression of feminine sensibility and/or repressed female sexuality. In a letter to Mitchell Kennerley, who directed several of her exhibitions, O'Keeffe wrote, "The things they write sound so strange and far removed from what I feel of myself. They make me seem like some strange unearthly sort of creature floating in the air—breathing in clouds for nourishment—when the truth is that I like beef steak—and like it rare at that" (Cowart 170-171).

110, Like an Early Blue Abstraction
Painting: Anonymous Collection, Charleston, VA IAP 8981079
The painting was done by O'Keeffe and John Poling, a gardener who later helped her with paintings. The epigraph is from Jill Krementz's *New York Social Diary* about an exhibition of O'Keeffe's abstractions at the Whitney Museum of American Art, September 17, 2009–January 17, 2010.

113, May 6, 1986

Though O'Keeffe lived in Santa Fe in the last years of her life, the bells rang from St. Thomas the Apostle in Abiquiu on the evening of her death (Lisle 437-438). She was cremated and her ashes were scattered, in accordance with her wishes, from the top of Pedernal Mountain.

AUTHOR'S ACKNOWLEDGEMENTS

These poems were made possible by the work of those who preceded me in exploring the lives and legacies of O'Keeffe and Stieglitz, including Sarah Greenough, for her insightful essays and expert curation of the O'Keeffe-Stieglitz correspondence; Eumie Imm-Stroukoff and Elizabeth Ehrnst, at the O'Keeffe Museum Research Center, for accommodating my novice approach to the archive (as well as the patient guards who opened all those drawers); and especially Laurie Lisle, both for writing *Portrait of an Artist*, the brilliant biography from which I culled the narrative arc of this collection, and for her generosity in reading and responding so positively to these poems.

I began this book while at Purdue University and am thankful to many there: Donald Platt, I owe much to your friendship and artful editing; Bich Minh Nguyen, for helping me sit comfortably between genres; Kristina Bross and Susan Curtis, for the tools and confidence needed to burrow into archives; Marianne Boruch, Wendy Flory, Patricia Henley, Maren Linett, Aparajita Sagar, Porter Shreve, and Sharon Solwitz, for your knowledge and support. For much useful advice, thanks to Visiting Writers Nicole Cooley, Bill Roorbach, Mary Szybist, and Natasha Trethewey. Gratitude, too, to my fellow writers for helpful suggestions on this work: Lindsey Alexander, Greg Allendorf, Brianne Carpenter, Julie Henson, Allison Hutchcraft, Matt Kilbane, Kara Krewer, Bethany Leach, Natalie Lund, Katie McClendon, Rebecca McKanna, Emily Skaja, and Natalie van Hoose.

And I have great gratitude for the teachers who bolstered me along the way, including David Ball, Jack Gilbert, Tabetha Ewing, Michael Gorra, Andrea Hairston, Marie Ponsot, Fran Rodgers, Teresa Tinsley, Marina Van Zuylen, Paula Varsano, Kurt Vonnegut, and especially Eleanor Wilner—thank you for your generous guidance, humor, and aide at every important juncture.

Robert Alexander, this went from manuscript to book because of you. Laure-Anne Bosselaar, you helped launch the sequence that gave this collection its heart. Jessi Hempel, thank you for close readings and innumerable insights. And much appreciation to generous readers Ariel Agai, Christopher Merrill, Susan Minot, Mary Molinary, Sarah Paley, and Elizabeth Schmidt, as well as editors Jody Bolz, Allison Funk, Michael Palmer, Jill Patterson, John Rosenwald, Lee Sharkey, and Rhett Iseman Trull.

And to the maintainers of my sanity amid the windfields, thank you: Sarah Davis, James Durett, Parrissa Eyorokon, Kristin Griffin, Terry Jones, Rebekah Jordan, Nina LaCour & Kristyn Stroble, Terrance L. Manning, Jr., Claire Michie, Amy Obermeyer, Lauren Perkins, Frank & Mary Shroff, Michael Shroff, Katie Storey, and Corey Van Landingham.

To those who kindly shared their homes: Mary Lou Mooney; Dennis Maloney & Elaine LaMattina; Katie Mead & Robert Alexander; and most vital of all, David Rice and Andrew & Elizabeth Sebastian—Gallina Canyon is one of the finest places I have known; these poems could not have been written anywhere else. Carolyn Metzler, thank you for sharing your love of Jacal and the hard-earned wisdom that allowed me to make it through my time there.

Dennis and Elaine, thank you for giving this book such a good home at White Pine Press.

For ceaseless love and support: my parents, to whom this book is dedicated; my sisters Jill and Nicole and mother-in-law Lisa Brown, for enthusiasm and sass; and my grandparents, Bernice Jacobs, the sharpest wit in South Florida, and the late Leo Jacobs, and the late Gloria and William Goodman, your generosity and integrity are the sightlines by which I guide my life. Nickole Brown, my wife, I would give anything to have sent you the right letter sooner; every word I write is for you.

THE AUTHOR

Jessica Jacobs grew up in Central Florida and has since lived in San Francisco and New York, with stints in Greece, Indiana and Arkansas along the way. Her work has appeared in *Beloit Poetry Journal, Cave Wall, Iron Horse, The Missouri Review, Poet Lore,* and *Rattle,* among other journals and anthologies. She holds a B.A. from Smith College and an M.F.A. from Purdue University. An avid long-distance runner, Jessica has worked as a rock climbing instructor, bartender, textbook Acquisitions Editor, Editor-in-Chief of *Sycamore Review,* and as the 2014–15 Visiting Asistant Professor of English at Hendrix College. She lives with her wife, the poet Nickole Brown. *Pelvis With Distance* is her debut collection.

Acknowledgments (continued from copyright page)

Connotations Press: An Online Artifact: "Red Barn in Wheatfield," "Untitled (Dead Rabbit with Copper Pot," and "No. 8—Special (Palo Duro Canyon with Spiral)"
Cutbank: "Music—Pink and Blue II," "Alfred Stieglitz (Self-Portrait in Absentia)," "Composite [Self-] Portrait as Wise Desert Elder," and "Georgia O'Keeffe, by Alfred Stieglitz (Composite Portrait)"
Flyway: Journal of Writing & Environment: "Coney Island, 1917" and "Lake George, 1922"
Iron Horse Literary Review: "Plate 28 (Clothed in Only a Swim Cap)," "Pelvis with Distance," "July 13, 1946"
The Journal: "Nude Series VII"
The Missouri Review: "The White Place in Shadow"
Overplay/Underdone: An Anthology of Poetry in the Third Dimension, edited by Patricia Flint and Ǽleen Frisch, (Medusa's Laugh Press, 2013): Sections of "In the Canyon IV (Reflections)," published as "Composing Ourselves"
poemmemoirstory: "Black Abstraction"
Poet Lore: "Early Abstraction"
Poetry Flash: "In the Patio IV (Green Door)" and "Once in Her Eighties Georgia Attempts a Joke"
Redivider: "May 6, 1986"
River Teeth: "In the Canyon VI (Hallucinations)," published as "Bells"
So to Speak: A Feminist Journal of Language and Art: "A Black-Bird with Snow-Covered Red Hills" and "From the Faraway, Nearby"
Sou'wester: "Georgia O'Keeffe (Half Naked, in White)," "Alfred Faces the Camera, Georgia Turns Away," and "Like an Early Blue Abstraction"

"A Black-Bird with Snow-Covered Red Hills" also appeared in *The Burden of Light: Poems on Illness and Loss,* edited by Tanya Chernov (Fast Foreword Publications, 2014).
"Lake George, 1922" was also published as a broadside, edited by Elizabeth Bradfield (Broadsided Press, 2015).
"July 13, 1946" also appeared on *Verse Daily.*